Mastering Options

Mastering Options

Effective and Profitable Strategies for Traders

Philip Cooper

BUSINESS EXPERT PRESS

First published in 2019 by
Business Expert Press, LLC
222 East 46th Street, New York, NY 10017
www.businessexpertpress.com

ISBN-13: 978-1-63157-907-3 (paperback)
ISBN-13: 978-1-63157-908-0 (e-book)

Business Expert Press Finance and Financial Management Collection

Collection ISSN: 2331-0049 (print)
Collection ISSN: 2331-0057 (electronic)

Cover and interior design by S4Carlisle Publishing Services Private Ltd., Chennai, India

First edition: 2019

10 9 8 7 6 5 4 3 2 1

Printed in the United States of America.

Dedication

This book is dedicated to my son Sammy Burton-Cooper, who has had exceptional patience with me over the years.

Abstract

If you are a beginner to the world of options, *Mastering Options—Effective and Profitable Strategies for Traders* is essential to learn the basics of option strategies that will enable you to start making consistently handsome earnings. This book gives the novice a comprehensive understanding of using option investment and hedging strategies successfully. It is primarily aimed at the undergraduate whose ambition is to either become a trader in a financial organization or an online investor through a financial broker's trading platform. It also provides seasoned investors and traders with new insights into using options as an investment tool. In simple-to-understand, concise language, enhanced by relevant graphics, the key trading tools available on online trading platforms are explained in enough detail that beginners will be able to understand as well as learn how to invest effectively in the financial markets using options. Chapter by chapter, this book builds a complete understanding of the basic building blocks of investing in options, including covering key charting techniques using technical tools.

Here's what you learn from *Mastering Options*:

- What options are in simple terms!
- The various types of options and the common terms used in options trading.
- The underlying principles of options trading using easily understandable scenarios.
- Insights into why you should trade in options.
- Strategies you can use to consistently make profits while continually monitoring your risk exposure.
- Case studies illustrating each strategy.

This book exposes the myth that investing in financial options is an impenetrable mystery.

Keywords

binary options; candlestick charts; CFD's; currency options; derivatives; financial markets; fundamental analysis; index options; stock options; straddles; strangles; technical analysis; trading

Contents

Acknowledgments

I wish to express gratitude to Nigel Wyatt of the Magenta Network and my publishers Business Expert Press for offering me the opportunity to write this book. Also to my good friend and ex-colleague Craig Abbott for his inspiration that started me down this writing road and another good friend Melvin Hurley whose mantra "keep smiling" kept me going when the going got tough.

My thanks to ex-colleagues who kindly edited the book for content— Gregory Matthews, David Evans, and Roger Francis. Many thanks for your time, guys.

Finally, gratitude to my partner Susan, who did not complain when I went missing for hours on end and was also my own personal grammatical editor who took a rough piece of work and made it flow.

CHAPTER 1

History of the Options Market

Before we delve into the history of options, it would be appropriate to look at the definition of an option.

Definition

Options are not financial instruments in themselves but are a financial derivative whose value is the underlying asset it represents. It represents a contract (an agreement) written by a seller (option writer) to a buyer (option holder), which offers the buyer the right but not the obligation to buy (call option) or sell (put option) a financial asset at a decided price (strike price) on a specific date (expiration date) in the future. In return for this right the option buyer pays a premium to the option writer.

A call option gives the buyer the right to buy an underlying asset in the hope that the price of the underlying asset will go up. The writer of a call option, however, would want the price to go down so that the option buyer would let the option expire without exercising it and the option writer would pocket the premium.

A put option is the opposite of a call option in that the buyer would want the underlying asset price to go down. However, the writer of the put option would want the underlying asset price to appreciate so that option buyer would let the option expire without exercise and the option writer pockets the premium paid.

Don't worry if you don't fully understand the concept yet, as a fuller explanation with many examples will be described in later chapters of this book.

History

You might think that options trading is a fairly new-fangled system of investment when compared to other more well known ways such as currency trading or buying and selling stocks. The modern-day options contracts were introduced in 1973 when the Chicago Board of Options Exchange was founded. However, the very first option to ever be transacted is said to have be in Ancient Greece by a businessman by the name of Thales in the mid-fourth century BC. Thales successfully created the first option contracts when he paid each owner of an olive press a sum of money to lock his right to use them at harvest time because, he had foreseen that the olive harvest would be the biggest in decades and consequently there would be a huge demand for them. The harvest was as Thales had predicted and he sold his rights to the olive presses to the farmers that needed them and made a large profit.

Although the term options was not in use, Thales had successfully created the first call option by paying for the right but not the obligation to use olive presses at a fixed price and he then exercised his option, gaining a fair profit. Thales had successfully executed a call option using olive presses as the underlying security.

Another important incident in the history of options occurred in the 17th century in Holland at the time of the "tulip bulb mania." Tulips at that time were immensely popular and the demand for them was increasing at a huge rate. Calls and puts were being extensively used during this period, not for speculation but for hedging purposes. Tulip wholesalers would buy calls to protect themselves from the price going up. Tulip growers would buy puts to protect themselves from the price going down. Contracts for calls and puts were not regulated or as established as they are today.

As the demand for tulip bulbs increased so did the price and therefore the value of the options contracts increased also. In addition, a secondary market emerged, which allowed anyone to speculate in the tulip bulb market. The price continued to rise as everyone invested in the market, until eventually the market could not sustain the high prices and the tulip bulb bubble burst and the price fell through the floor. Because the options market was not regulated, there was no authority to force investors to fulfill their obligations and many people lost their life's savings or their houses and the Dutch economy suffered as it went into recession. At that point in history, options had acquired a really bad reputation; however, they did still appeal to a lot of investors because of the leverage they possessed. Ultimately they could not overcome their bad name and were banned for 100 years from the 18th to the 19th century.

The next big development in the history of options happened in the late 19th century when a gentleman called Russell Sage started to create call and put options that could be traded over the counter (not through banks or an exchange). He created a lot of activity, which proved to be a noteworthy breakthrough in options trading. He also created formulas that enabled him to establish a relationship between the price of the underlying asset and the price of the option. Unfortunately he suffered substantial losses and was forced to stop trading but is still attributed to the advancement of options trading.

The trading of options continued through Put and Call Brokers and Dealers who advertised in an attempt to attract buyers and sellers so that the brokers could attempt to match buyers with sellers. Although this was an arduous process, it at least enabled the options market to increase in activity while remaining fairly illiquid. It was at this time that The Put and Calls Brokers and Dealers Association was formed to facilitate the establishment of networks that could help match buyers to sellers and also establish some sort of standards for options. Investors were a lot less wary than previously; however, the lack of regulation did not allow the options market to grow at any significant pace.

Throughout the early 20th century the options market continued to grow at a slow pace with more people becoming educated in options and their potential uses. However, there was still no pricing structure as such even though the Securities and Exchange Commission had introduced some regulation to the options market. It wasn't until 1970 that options became fully regulated when the Chicago Board of Trade introduced exchange traded options (1973) and provided a fair transparent marketplace for them to be traded. In addition, the Options Clearing Corporation was formed to establish a centralized clearing process and the proper fulfillment of trades. Also in 1973 two professors, Myron Scholes and Fisher Black, created their Black Scholes Pricing Model, which used a mathematical formula to calculate the price of an option using specific variables. These events made investors far more comfortable in trading options and finally legitimized options, over 2,000 years after Thales.

Today, with the advent of online trading in options, it has become accessible to many more investors and from a volume of 20,000 traded in 1974, the market has grown to the current volumes of millions traded each day covering thousands of different contracts over many financial assets. Options are extremely popular and show no sign of their growth slowing down.

So there we have it, history lesson over and welcome to the wonderful world of options! Options are possibly one of the most miscomprehended trading instruments on the financial market today. Which is one of the reasons behind this book—to simplify the rhetoric, eliminate the myths, and show you how options are a powerful tool for making money, and reducing risk, if used sensibly. If you understand what they are and how to use them, options are terrific! As we have already mentioned, there has never been a better time for the individual to make money from options.

The reasons for this are as follows:

1. The Internet offers access to real-time data, all the research you could wish for, and more material than you could ever hope to read in a lifetime.
2. Electronic trading has greatly reduced transactions costs.

Options permit through leverage and their limited risk, the ability to customize strategies that exactly align your investment strategies with the market environment, thus enabling you to keep control and retain the odds of profitability in your favor. Each option contract represents a multiple (usually 100) of the underlying asset but costs through its premium a fraction of the price you would pay for purchasing the underlying asset outright. This means that options can give you huge returns on moderately small price movements.

CHAPTER 2

Option Profit-and-Loss Diagrams

Call Options

The call option buyer (option holder) has the right but not the obligation to buy the underlying asset at the specified time in the future (expiration date) at a specified price (strike price). The call option writer has the obligation to sell the option if exercised at the specified price and date in return for a premium paid by the option buyer (Table 2.1).

Call Profit-and-Loss Diagrams

We will start with looking at the profit-and-loss diagram for the long call option. The long call is the position of the holder (buyer) of the call option. We will assume that you have purchased a call option on ABC stock at a strike price of $43 per share and paid a premium of $2 per share. In the real world of course one option would be a hundred shares, so your total premium would be $200. As you can see from Figure 2.1, your break-even price is $45 per share because you have paid the $2 per share premium.

Any price below your break-even price of $45 per share would be a loss and the option would be deemed out of the money. At a share price of $44 your loss is $1 per share, the strike price of $43 plus the $1 per

Table 2.1 Call option contract

Call option contract	
Call buyer	Call seller/writer
Has right	*Has Obligation*

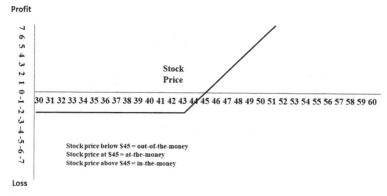

Figure 2.1 Long call option profit-and-loss diagram

share profit less the $2 premium you paid. At a share price at $43, the strike price, or below would leave you with the loss of the $2 premium per share. If the stock price was $45 on expiry date, the option would be deemed at the money, which is your break-even price. Any stock price above $45 per share would be profit for you and the option would be deemed in the money. As you can see from the diagram, your profit is unlimited but your loss is limited to the premium of $2 you paid per share. If the option was out of the money on the exercise date, you would simply let it expire as it has no value and take the loss of the premium you paid. However, if the option was in the money on the expiration date and the underlying share price was $50, the value of the option would reflect the profit you had made on the underlying share price and you could either sell the option and lock in your $7 profit, or you could purchase the underlying shares at the $43 per share strike price and sell the shares in the open market at $50 for a profit of $7 per share.

Now let's look at the option writer's side of the contract, which is called a short call. The option writer's profit-and-loss diagram, Figure 2.2, tells a very different story.

The diagram shows that the option writer makes a profit (the premium received) as long as the underlying share price remains below $45 per share. If the stock price is at $45 on the expiry date, the option writer breaks even. However, if the price per share is above $45, the option writer makes a loss. The potential losses for a short call option if the stock price goes up are unlimited for the option writer.

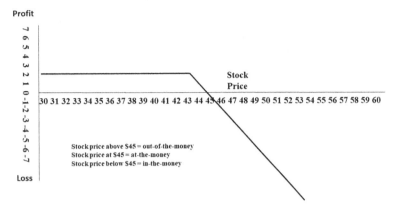

Figure 2.2 Short call option profit-and-loss diagram

Table 2.2 Put option contract

Put option contract	
Put buyer	Put seller/writer
Has right	Has obligation

Put Options

The put option buyer (option holder) has the right but not the obligation to buy the underlying asset at the specified time in the future (exercise date) at a specified price (strike price). The put option writer has the obligation to sell the option if exercised at the specified price and date in return for a premium paid by the option buyer (Table 2.2).

Put Profit-and-Loss Diagrams

Let's look at the profit-and-loss diagram for the long put option. The long put is the position of the holder (buyer) of the put option. Assume that you have purchased a put option on ABC stock at a strike price of $43 per share and paid a premium of $2 per share. As you can see from Figure 2.3, your break-even price is $41 per share because you have paid the $2 per share premium. At this price the option is deemed at the money.

Once the price has dropped below $41, your break-even price, the option is deemed to be in the money. However, if the underlying price is above $41, the option is deemed out of the money and the option buyer

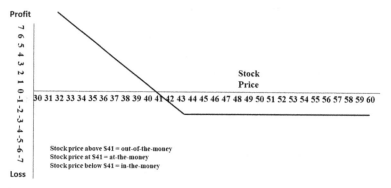

Figure 2.3 Long put option profit-and-loss diagram

only loses the premium paid ($2 per share) to the option writer no matter how far above $41 the underlying price moves. For the long put option buyer, losses are limited to the premium paid; however, the profits are unlimited.

The other side of the long put option is the short put option. This is the position of the option writer and the profit-and-loss diagram for this position is shown in Figure 2.4.

Figure 2.4 shows that the option writer makes a profit (the premium received) as long as the underlying share price remains above $43 per share (in the money). If the underlying stock price is at $43 on the expiry date, the option writer breaks even (option is at the money). However, if the price per share is below $43, the option writer makes a loss (out of the money). The potential losses for a short put option if the stock price goes up are unlimited for the option writer.

As we have seen, an option has two parts; the holder or buyer of the option and the opposite part is the option writer. Now let's summarize what we know about options so far (Table 2.3).

We shall see in later chapters how we can take advantage of those option characteristics to create profitable option strategies.

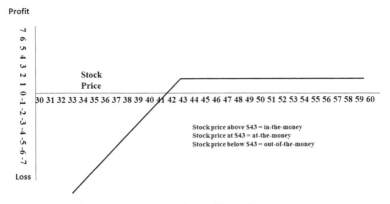

Figure 2.4 Short put option profit-and-loss diagram

Table 2.3 Option contract types and their characteristics

Option type	Limited profit	Limited loss	Unlimited profit	Unlimited loss
Long call	No	Yes	Yes	No
Short call	Yes	No	No	Yes
Long put	No	Yes	Yes	No
Short put	Yes	No	No	Yes

CHAPTER 3

Types of Options

There are several different types of options, which have the characteristics that we have outlined in the previous chapter; however, there some options that have slightly different characteristics and one particular type—the binary option—which is very different from other options. Options are categorized in classes as follows:

American Type Option: This term refers to how the option is exercised. An American option can be exercised at any time during the life of the contract. It could be exercised a few days after the contract is opened or at any time before the expiration date. These options are the most used in today's markets and all the examples of options in this book are American type options.

European Type Option: This option gives the option holder the right to only exercise the option on the specified expiration date. For example, you might have a European option that gives you the right to buy 100 ABC shares on June 15 at $5.00 per share. The price rises between now and May 19 and reaches $10.00 per share, but you cannot exercise your option until June 15. By the time June 15 arrives, the stock is only worth $2.00 per share. Now you will have to let your option expire worthless.

Barrier Option: This option has a component in addition to the strike price and the expiry date. This component is called a *trigger*. The trigger or barrier price, if reached, either opens the options contract (knocks in) and makes it a regular options contract or cancels the option contract (knocks out) and the contract is never taken up. These options are cheaper than plain vanilla options because in many cases these options never materialize.

Binary Options: These are very simple to use and trade. The reason they are called binary or digital options is that when you trade them you only have two decisions to make, either a 0 or a 1. It's a bit like flipping a coin, you can call heads or tails, and there is no other option available to you. This is the same for the binary option; its future price is either going to be *up* or its going to be *down*. What could be simpler than that? This is what makes the binary option an excellent and easy way for a novice trader to get into the global trading markets and trade currencies, stocks, commodities, or stock indices.

The binary option is not always traded in the same way and investors have access to several different methods of trading them.

The *High/Low* method is sometimes called the Up/Down or the Call/Put method. This is the most basic type of binary options trade. With this trade, you choose an asset, that might be a stock, currency, commodity, or index, and you decide whether the asset will be trading at a price that is higher or lower than the current price at a chosen expiry time. If you believe the answer is *higher*, you simply pick *High* on the binary options platform you trade on (or *Up* or *Call*). If you believe the answer is *lower*, you then pick *Low* on your platform (or *Down* or *Put*). Figure 3.1 shows a $10 GBP/USD binary options possible trade. The strike price is 1.4070 with expiry in three hours from now (11:50). If you decide that GBP/USD will go higher, you will click on the purchase button for higher. Some platforms use Call/Put terminology. If GBP/USD is higher on expiry, you will get a 81.9 percent return on your investment. So you

Figure 3.1 High/low GBP/USD trade

will receive $18.9, which is your initial investment of $10 plus profit of $8.19. If you decided that GBP/USD would be lower after 3 hours, you would click on the purchase button for lower. The return on investment if you won this trade would be 81.7 percent. If you lose a binary options trade you lose 100 percent of your initial investment. In this case $10.

The expiry times can vary, or they can be set by you on some platforms, which is a more customizable form of High/Low trading offered by some binary options brokers. Expiry times range widely, but for High/Low trades it will usually range from 5 to 15 minutes to sometime hours later on the same day. However, more and more binary options brokers are offering longer term expiry times ranging from 1 week to 1 month or even 6 months.

The **One Touch/No Touch** trading method works a little differently than high/low trading. With one touch/no touch trading, you are looking at a given asset, and you are deciding if the asset will reach (one touch) or not reach (no touch) a specific price point by the expiry date.

This price point may be anywhere between the current price and the price on the expiry date. Usually the further away the price point is from the current price level, the higher your potential payout if you win. A price point that is located nearby is easier to reach, and therefore would pay out less since the risk is lower. If you say that the asset will touch the price point, and it does, anytime within the expiry period, you win your trade and the payout. If you are wrong, you lose your investment. However, you can also decide that the asset will not touch the price point during the duration of the time frame. If you say that the asset will not touch a specific price point, and it doesn't anytime within the time period, you win the trade. If it does touch, you lose. Figure 3.2 below shows a typical one touch/no touch trade.

As you can see, one touch/no touch trades typically offer much higher payouts than other binary trades. This is because there is more risk connected with them. Whereas the average payout for high/low trades might be near to 85 percent, for one touch trades your broker might offer you payouts in the 300 percent range or more. The one touch part of the trade shown in Figure 3.2 has a very low return (7.8 percent) because over the time period of 67 days it is highly likely that the price will reach the 1.4088 price point. On the other hand, on the no touch side of the trade,

Figure 3.2 One touch/no touch GBP/USD trade

the risk is high that you will lose, as it is likely that the 1.4088 will be touched during the 67 days and so the return is very high at 558.7 percent.

The **Boundary** method trades are like the aforementioned binary option trading methods, easy to execute and understand. However, as with all trading you should do your homework (analysis) and have developed your trading strategy, which frequently means that the strategy behind placing winning trades is quite complex.

The basics of the boundary trade are that you have to predict whether the price of the asset will be within a given range at expiry or that it will be outside a given range at expiry. You decide which asset to trade, the dollar amount of your trade, the boundary range, the expiry time, and whether you think the price will finish inside or outside of the broker's range.

In Figure 3.3 the boundary is between USD/CHF 0.94168 and USD/CHF 0.93474 (the prices form the outside barriers) and the expiry is 11 days from today. If you choose an inside boundary option, your trade will expire in the money if the USD/CHF price ends within the range determined by you. If the price at the expiry time is outside the range, you'll lose the funds ($10) you staked for your position. Notice that your return on your stake is 245.5 percent if your prediction of the price finishing within the range is correct. The reason the return is so high is that you are taking a greater risk predicting the price will be within the range than predicting it will be outside the range. The option runs for 11 days with the barriers being only 69 pips apart. The chances of the price staying within the boundary are very slim. However, if you choose to predict that the price will be outside the range, your chances of winning are very good

Figure 3.3 Boundary USD/CHF trade

and that is reflected in the return you will get if the price finished as you predicted. A measly 22.6 percent.

One definite way to lose money when range trading is to implement trades without doing any research or having any data about the underlying asset's market. Unless you have at least a rudimentary understanding of the factors that affect an asset's value, you'll find it tough to execute profitable trades on a reliable basis. And as we have said before, this is the case with all binary option types.

The **Ladder** method is a more recent type of binary option and is also more complex than the other methods we have mentioned. This method offers various returns on your investment during the life of the option. The name Ladder suggests the *interval* aspect of the strike prices involved. This particular trade enables you to take partial profits if your trade only goes part of the way to the set strike price. Furthermore, you have a chance to win more profits if the price moves further.

With a Ladder trade, you choose an asset, and there are three different strike prices and three different expiry times that are set by your broker's platform. As the asset progresses through the strike prices (like the rungs on a Ladder), you are given a certain partial payout percentage.

Let's say you are trading GBP/USD. The current price level is 1.3913. The current time is 09.00 a.m.

These strike prices and expiry times are set:

Table 3.1 Ladder prices

Strike	Strike price	Time (a.m.)	Payout (%)
1	1.3920	09.05	35
2	1.3925	09.10	40
3	1.3930	09.15	70
4	1.3950	09.20	95
5	1.3960	09.25	125

The payouts set by your broker's binary options platform will normally reflect how risky your trade is determined to be. For the nearer strike prices within a short time frame, your broker will offer you smaller payouts. If the strike prices are further apart with a longer time period to expiry, you are essentially predicting a greater move, and you would probably be offered much higher payouts.

In the previous example, you are trading GBP/USD, and you are predicting it will rise, your trade would have to progress along the *rungs* of your Ladder as follows:

Table 3.2 Ladder progression

Time (a.m.)	GBP/USD price	In/out/at the money	Potential payout (%)
09.05	1.3921	In	35
09.10	1.3925	At	40
09.15	1.3920	In	70
09.20	1.3953	In	95
09.25	1.3960	At	125

If you add up all those payouts, you get a total payout percentage of 365 percent. Remember, the percentages offered will depend on the perceived risk of your investment as your broker analyzes it. If your Ladder trade is too *easy* to achieve, you will be offered only small payouts. If, however, your Ladder trade is too *difficult*, and has no basis in reality, you are not going to win.

We shall look at different strategies for successfully trading binary options in a later chapter.

CHAPTER 4

Exchange-Traded Options

Exchange-Traded Options are options traded on a regulated exchange where the terms of every option are standardized by the exchange. The contract is standardized in a way that the underlying asset, quantity, expiration date, and strike price are known to all parties in advance. When options are in the money or at the money, they are characteristically exercised and settled through a clearinghouse.

The characteristics of exchange-traded options are:

- All the option terms are standardized except for the price.
- The exchange will establish the expiration date and expiration prices as well as minimum price quotation unit.
- The exchange will also establish if the option is American or European.
- The exchange will establish contract size and if settlement is in cash or in the underlying security.
- Options are usually traded in lots in which 100 shares of a stock = 1 option.
- Exchange-traded options usually have short-term expirations of 1 to 6 months duration.
- Options can be bought and sold easily and the holder decides whether or not to exercise.
- When options are in the money or at the money they are typically exercised.
- Most have to deliver the underlying security.
- They are regulated at the federal level in the US and by the FCA in the UK and Europe.

The underlying assets for exchange-traded options usually are:

- **Stocks (stock options)** are also known as equity options, these are agreements sold by one party to another. Stock options give the buyer the right, but not the obligation, to buy (call) or sell (put) a stock at an agreed upon price during a certain period of time or on a specific date.

- **Commodities (commodity options)** are options in which the underlying asset is a commodity such as wheat, gold, oil, and soybeans.

- **Bonds (bond options)** are option contracts in which the underlying asset is a bond. There is no significant difference between stock and bond options other than the different characteristics between the two assets. Just as with other options, a bond option permits investors to hedge the risk of their bond portfolios or gamble on the direction of bond prices with limited risk profile. A buyer of a bond call option is expecting a decline in interest rates and an increase in bond prices. The buyer of a put bond option is expecting an increase in interest rates and a decrease in bond prices.

- **Stock Market Indices (index options)** are call or put options on a financial index, such as the Nasdaq, S&P 500, or FTSE100. Investors trading index options are essentially predicting the overall movement of the stock market as represented by the basket of stocks in the index.

- **Options on futures** are options on a futures contract where the option holder has the right but not the obligation, to buy or sell a specific futures contract at a specific price on or before a certain expiration date. These grant the right to enter into a futures contract at a fixed price.

- **Forex (currency options)** is a contract that gives the holder the right, but not the obligation, to buy (call) or sell (put) currency at a specified price during a specified period of time. Investors generally use these types of option to hedge against their foreign currency risk by purchasing a currency option put or call.

CHAPTER 5

Over-the-Counter Options

Over-the-counter options are options traded between two parties that are nonstandardized so that the option can be tailored for any business or individual need. Most of the time one of the parties, and it's usually the writer of the option, is a well-capitalized institution such as a bank or an online broker. The option types that are mainly traded over the counter are:

- Stocks (stock options)
- Forex (currency options)
- Stock market (index options)
- Binary options

These are the types of options that you will be able to trade on your chosen online brokers platform.

Trading Stock Options

Stock options can be traded on most online brokers' platforms. As with all trading, before you trade with your own money, make sure that you understand the characteristics of stock options and the fundamentals that drive a stocks price. The trading screen for a stock option will look very similar to the screen shown in Table 5.1.

Let's assume that the market price of a Facebook share is $180 and you believe that the share price will appreciate over the next 30 days. To potentially take advantage of your belief, you decide to buy 10 call option contracts at the price of $5.98 each. The price is the premium per contract you pay for the right to buy Facebook shares at a strike price of $185 per share. As each option contract is worth 100 of the underlying Facebook

Table 5.1 Stock option trade

Stock	Market price	Trade date	Strike price	Expiry date	Call/put	Sell	Buy	Contracts	Contracts value
Facebook	$180	19th Sep	$185	18th Oct	Call	5.84	5.98	10	$598.00

shares, you have effectively bought the right but not the obligation to buy 100 Facebook contracts before or on the 18th October at a cost of $598 instead of a cost of $180,000 (10 contracts × 100 shares × $180) for purchasing the shares for cash.

Let's look at what happens if the price of Facebook shares do the opposite of what you expected and fall to $178 per share (out of the money). You would let the option expire worthless and forfeit the premium you paid of $598 (Table 5.2). If you had purchased the 1,000 shares for cash at the market price of $180 per share instead of purchasing the call option, you would have lost $2 per share for a total of $2,000. So by purchasing the call options you reduced your potential losses by $1,402 (Table 5.3).

However, if before or on 18th October the price of Facebook shares has increased in value to say $188 per share (in the money), you could exercise the option at the strike price of $185 per share giving you a profit of 10 × 100 × $3 = $3,000 less the premium you paid of $598, leaving you with a profit of $2,402 on the trade.

Table 5.4 is an example of the option exercised in the money on or before expiry. You don't actually have to buy the shares at the strike price and then sell them into the market at the market price to realize your profit. It is assumed that this is a given so the option writer (the seller) will always pay you your profit less the premium you paid him at inception of the contract.

Of course if you predict that Facebook stock would decline in the coming months and you wanted to hedge your risk you would purchase a put option. The workings would be similar except that instead of the price needing to be above the strike price to make a profit, with a put option it needs to be below the strike price (Table 5.5).

Table 5.2 Call stock option trade allowed to expire (out of the money)

Instru-ment	Strike price	Contracts	Expiry date	Call/put	Underlying stock price at expiry	Loss is premium paid
Facebook	$185	10	18th Oct	Call	$178	$598

Table 5.3 Facebook stocks purchased for cash

Instru-ment	Share price	Shares	Share price at Oct 18th	Potential loss per share	Total poten-tial loss	Potential reduction on losses
Facebook	$180	1,000	$178	$2	$2,000	$1,402

Table 5.4 Call stock option trade exercised (in the money)

Instrument	Strike price	Contracts	Expiry date	Call/put	Underlying stock price at expiry	Profit per share	Net Profit after options exercised
Facebook	$185	10	18th Oct	Call	$188	$3	$2,402

Table 5.5 Put stock option trade exercised (in the money)

Instrument	Strike price	Contracts	Expiry date	Call/put	Underlying stock price at expiry	Profit per share	Net profit after options exercised
Facebook	$185	10	18th Oct	Put	$182	$3	$2,402

Now, what if you were the writer of the Facebook call option expiring on the 18th October with a strike price of $185 and not the purchaser of the call? As a writer you would want the opposite result of the purchasers prediction and be hoping that the call option would expire worthless so you could pocket the premium of $598, which would be your profit. The call option would expire worthless only if the buyer's call option was out of the money on the expiry date (Table 5.6).

Table 5.6 Writer's side of call stock option allowed to expire (out of the money)

Instrument	Strike price	Contracts	Expiry date	Call/put	Underlying stock price at expiry	Profit per share	Net Profit after options expire
Facebook	$185	10	18th Oct	Call	$182	$3	$598

Table 5.7 Writer's side of call stock option exercised (in the money)

Instrument	Strike price	Contracts	Expiry date	Call/put	Underlying stock price at expiry	Profit per share	Net loss after options exercised
Facebook	$185	10	18th Oct	Call	$182	$3	$2,402

However, as a writer if the stock option was exercised in the money, it would cost you the $3,000 you would have to pay to the buyer of the option, less the premium of $598 you received from the buyer at the inception of the option contract, leaving you with a net loss of $2,402 (Table 5.7).

Not quite your shirt but significant nevertheless.

Stock options can be used for speculation on the direction of the market as in the examples in Table 5.7 or as a hedging tool. An example of a hedge is where you had a long stock position in ABC shares and was not sure where the market was going but didn't want to sell the shares. You could open a long put position to match the number of shares held. In this way if the market went down, the loss on the shares you held would be matched by the gain made on the "in the money" put options. In this case a perfect hedge. However, if the market continued to gain, all you would lose is the premium paid for the put options purchased.

Table 5.8 Option strategy

Option Type	Strategy
Buy call	Bullish
Buy put	Bearish
Sell/write put	Bullish
Sell/write call	Bearish

Trading Foreign Currency Options

Foreign Currency options have the same characteristics as other options that are tradable in the over-the-counter markets, such as stocks and indices. Most currency option contracts are traded over the counter with little regulation but a few contracts are traded on exchanges that are highly regulated. Over-the-counter options can be traded through a broker's trading platform. Foreign currency options are slightly different from traditional options in that with traditional options you pay for the right to buy or sell a given underlying asset, but with a currency option you buy or sell the right to an underlying asset denominated in another currency.

As we have mentioned earlier, there are four positions that you can take depending on your options strategy and whether you are bullish or bearish on a particular asset (Table 5.8).

Long Call

For example, suppose you were bullish on the price of the USD/CAD. You decide to buy a long call at a strike price of USD/CAD 1.2300 paying a premium of USD 0.005/CAD with an expiry date 2 months into the future. At expiry, you will not exercise the call if the spot rate is below USD/CAD 1.2300 because the long call would be out of the money. You would, however, exercise the call if the spot rate is above USD/CAD 1.2300 (in the money). The break-even point is at the spot rate of USD/CAD 1.2350. If the spot rate is USD/CAD 1.2450, you purchase the USD/CAD at the strike price of USD/CAD 1.2300 and sell them on the current spot market at a rate of USD/CAD 1.2450. Because you paid a premium of USD 0.005/CAD, you earn a profit of USD 0.01 per CAD purchased (Table 5.9). For this transaction the profits can be computed as:

Table 5.9 *Option long call profit calculation*

Spot rate	−	Strike price + premium	=	Profit/pips
1.2450	−	(1.2300 + 0.005) = 1.2350	=	0.0100

So your overall profit if you had bought a standard lot of 100 options (typical size 1,000 units of base currency) would be 100 × 1,000 × 0.0100 = $1,000 less the premium you paid of 100 × 1,000 × 0.005 = $500, which leaves you with a net profit of $500.

However, if the spot price was below USD/CAD 1.2300 at expiry and you would simply let the option expire without exercising it, and you would only lose the premium you paid of USD 0.005/CAD or $500.

So, as you have seen, the profit potential for a long call is unlimited and the potential loss is limited to no more than the premium paid.

Short Call

On the other hand, if you were the writer of the above call (short call), you would be hoping that the spot rate at maturity is out of the money, in other words, below USD/CAD 1.2300 (the strike price). As we have seen in Table 5.8, the payoffs to the writer are the opposite of the pay-off to the holder. In other words, the premium − (spot rate − strike price) = profit. For the writer of the call the potential gain is limited to the premium but the potential loss is infinite.

Long Put

Let's look at another strategy. Suppose you were bearish on the price of the USD/CHF but didn't want to take the risk of entering a straightforward forex transaction and being wrong on the outcome. So you decide to buy a USD/CHF long put. This is a gamble that the spot rate at maturity is below the strike price (you are selling the US dollar).

You purchase a put option contract on the USD/CHF at a strike price of USD/CHF 0.9950 (at the money option) and pay a premium of USD 0.004/CHF. At maturity, you would not exercise the option if the spot rate is above USD/CHF 0.9950. However, you would exercise the option if the spot rate is below USD/CHF 0.9950. The break-even point is the spot rate of USD/CHF 0.9910. If the spot rate is USD/CHF 0.9840

Table 5.10 Long put option profit calculation

Strike price	–	Spot rate + premium	=	Profit/pips
0.9950	–	(0.9840 + 0.004) = 0.9880	=	0.007

when the option is due to expire, you buy the USD/CHF on the current spot market at the rate of USD/CHF 0.9840 and sell them at the strike price of USD/CHF 0.9950. As you paid a premium of USD 0.004/CHF, you will earn a profit of USD 0.007 per CHF sold (Table 5.10). For this transaction the profits can be computed as.

As with the long call, the potential gain is unlimited but the maximum loss is only the premium you paid.

Short Put

However, if you were the writer of the above put, you would be betting that the spot rate is above the strike price at maturity. As we can see from Table 5.8, the payoffs to the put writer are the exact opposite to the holder of a long put because the writer's profit is the premium when the option is left to expire and not exercised. That is, premium – (strike price – spot rate) = profit. As with a short call your potential gain is limited to the premium and the maximum loss is unlimited.

There are essentially only two currency option strategies you could employ:

1. Speculating on the price action of the currency spot market.
2. Hedging an open currency position.

The examples we have discussed earlier are straightforward speculative strategies; however, a hedging strategy is slightly more complicated. To hedge a position you have to open an opposite currency option position to the spot position you hold.

For example, if you held a long spot currency position, you would open a long put currency option to match the value of the spot currency position held. If your long spot position gained value in your favor, you would allow the long put to expire worthless, so your net profit would be the increase in value of your long spot position less the premium you paid for the long put. If the value of your long spot position fell, the loss on that position would be offset by the gains you made on your long put.

Let's assume you are holding a GBP/USD long spot position at a spot rate of GBP/USD 1.3430 and you believe that the GBP/USD will increase in value over the next couple of months. To hedge your spot position you would purchase a 2 month long put GBP/USD currency option to match the exact value of your spot currency position, with a strike price of GBP/USD 1.3430, paying a premium of GBP 0.0020/USD. If at the maturity date of the long put option the spot price of GBP/USD is higher than GBP/USD 1.3450, (spot price 1.3430 + 0.0020 premium paid) you would allow the long put to expire worthless and sell your spot position and take your profit. However, if the value of your spot currency position had fallen below 1.3430 to, for example, 1.3400 (a loss of GPB 0.0030/USD), you would exercise the long put option and sell GBP/USD at 1.3430 (the strike price) and purchase GBP/USD in the spot market at GBP/USD 1.3400, making a profit of 1.3430 (strike price) − 1.3400 (spot price) + 0.0020 (premium paid) = 0.0010 profit. This profit would partially offset the reduction in value of your spot position at GBP/USD 1.3400, (a loss of GBP 0.0030/USD) and you would end up making an overall loss of GBP 0.0020/USD, a far better result than taking a risk on your spot position without hedging it.

Trading Stock Index Options

Index options are the same as stock options, except the underlying asset is a stock/share index instead of a single stock. An index call or put option is a simple and popular tool used by investors, traders, and speculators to profit on the general direction of an underlying index while putting very little capital at risk. The profit potential for long index call options is unlimited, while the risk is limited to the premium amount paid for the option, regardless of the index level at expiration. For long index put options, the risk is also limited to premium paid, and the potential profit is topped at the index level, less the premium paid, as the index can never go below zero.

Exactly like any call option, an index call option gives the owner the right to buy the underlying index at a future date at a specified price. For this privilege the index call owner pays the writer of the call a premium. Similarly, just like any put option, an index put option gives the owner the right to sell the underlying index at a future date at a specified price. For this privilege the index put option owner pays a premium to the put option writer. Once owned, you have the choice of whether you want to exercise the option and take a position on the underlying asset. If the current market index price is lower than the strike price for a call or the market index price is higher than the strike price for a put, you can simply let the option expire worthless.

Most online broker platforms facilitate the trading of stock index options and you should choose the one that meets your own personal trading goals. The platforms that facilitate index options normally have the major stock indices as tradable assets, although some do allow trading the lesser indices. The most popular indices for trading index options are listed in Table 5.11.

Take a look at Table 5.12 for an example of a typical trading platform's index option screen.

The first column shows index option SPX, which is the designation for the underlying asset Standard & Poor's Index. The second column shows an array of strike prices. The third column is the expiry month for the option. The fourth column designates whether the strike price is for a put or

Table 5.11 Popular Indices

Index	Country
Standard & Poor's 500	USA
Dow Jones 30	USA
NASDAQ	USA
FTSE 100	UK
DAX	Germany
Hang Seng	Hong Kong
CAC 40	France
Nikkei 500	Japan
FTSE MID 250	UK
Russel 3000	USA

Table 5.12 Index options screenshot

Index	Strike price	Expiry date	Put/call	Sell/write premium	Buy premium
SPX	2,480	Oct	Call	35.72	36.52
SPX	2,480	Oct	Put	14.59	15.16
SPX	2,490	Oct	Call	28.20	28.80
SPX	2,490	Oct	Put	16.92	17.57
SPX	2,500	Oct	Call	24.08	25.41
SPX	2,500	Oct	Put	14.48	15.56

a call. The fifth column is the premium on the sell/write side of the option. The sixth column indicates the premium on the buy side of the option.

Index Option Long Call Example

You observe that the current value of the S&P 500 is at the 2,490 level. You believe that the index will rise over the next weeks so you decide to buy an SPX long call with a strike price as near to the current price as possible. You choose the strike price of 2,500, which has a premium of $25.41 and an expiry date in October a few weeks from now. With a contract multiplier of 100, the premium you have to pay to hold the call option is $2,541. On the expiration date the underlying S&P 500 index has risen by 5 percent and stood at 2,614.50. With the S&P Index significantly higher than the strike price, the option is very much in the money. You exercise the option and receive a cash settlement figure that is computed as follows. ($2,614.50 expiration price − $2,500 strike price) × 100 = $11,450 from the option transaction. Deduct the premium of $2,541 and your net profit is $8,909 from the long call strategy. As with the settling of all option contracts, it is not necessary to exercise the option to take your profit, you can simply close out the option by selling it back into the market.

The obvious advantage from the long call strategy is that your loss is limited to a known specific amount but your profits are unlimited. If the S&P 500 had fallen by 5 percent to 2,375 instead of rising, which is a long way from the strike price of 2,500, you would have only lost $2,541, the cost of your premium paid.

A long put strategy on the same index option would work in exactly the same way as the long call strategy except that you would want to see the underlying asset fall below the strike price to make a profit. If the underlying asset rose above the strike price, you would lose the premium you had paid. Writing or selling put and call index options exposes you to the possibility of unlimited losses if you get it wrong. Recall that when writing or selling a put index option, your expectation is that the underlying asset will rise above the strike price. Conversely, when writing a call index option you are expecting the underlying price to fall below the strike price.

Keep in mind that long call or put strategies can lead to unlimited profits but limited losses if you get it wrong; however, short call or put strategies can lead to limited profits but unlimited losses if the market goes against you.

CHAPTER 6

Profitable Strategies for Binary Option Trading

There are many strategies for you to consider when you contemplate investing in binary options. You have a choice of short-, medium-, or long-term strategies the use of which depends on how comfortable you are with trading different time frames. If you have been trading forex previous to trying your hand at binary options, you should keep to the time frames you have been trading so as to remain in your comfort zone. As with trading forex or stocks, binary options strategies incorporate the use of the same technical analysis tools and indicators that you would have been accustomed to when trading stocks or forex.

Charts

Charts are an integral part of technical analysis and if you have been trading stocks or forex you should be quite familiar with the various types of charts and you can skip this section and move onto binary option strategies. If, however, you are new to charting, you should complete this section before moving on.

The most basic chart is the *line chart*. The line chart consists of adjacent lines that connect all the closing prices of each time period together. Figure 6.1 presents a one day period line chart for the USD/CHF currency pair.

As you can see from the line chart in Figure 6.1, it shows the level of currency closing prices but does not give you any other information. You can see how the price fluctuates over a period of time, in this case a series of daily periods covering several months. This is not a popular chart as it doesn't give you enough information to enable you to execute a successful strategy.

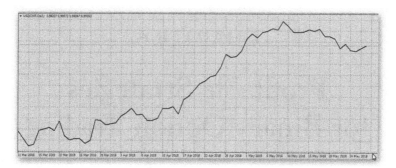

Figure 6.1 USD/CHF daily line chart

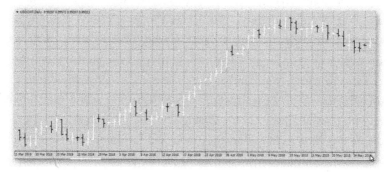

Figure 6.2 USD/CHF daily bar chart

A second type of chart is the *bar chart* (Figure 6.2); this chart displays much more information than the line chart. It displays the closing and opening prices, plus the highest price and the lowest price of the day. This is the second most popular chart with traders that use a technical analysis approach to trading. The chart also displays time periods with each bar representing a specific time period.

The length of each bar shows the two extremes of the price action for the time period; the top of the bar shows the highest price and the bottom of the bar shows the lowest price. The left-hand-side tag shows the opening price for that period and the right-hand tag shows the closing price. Notice how much more information there is on the above chart compared to the line chart.

The most popular and most used chart of all is the candlestick chart. This chart has the same information as the bar chart; however, it also gives

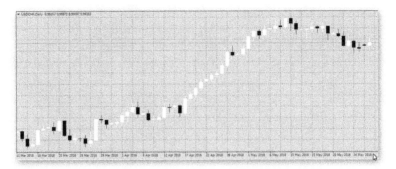

Figure 6.3 USD/CHF daily candlestick chart

information about the strength of the buyers and sellers. The candlesticks themselves have bodies and wicks as shown in the candlestick chart in Figure 6.3.

The black solid candles represent prices that are falling and the top of the body represents the opening price, the bottom of the body the closing price, and the extremes of the wicks the period high (top of the wick) and the period low price (bottom of the wick). The white solid candles represent a rising price, the period high and low are represented by the wicks but the body now indicates the opening price at its bottom and the closing price at its top. Furthermore, the length of the top and bottom wicks (shadows) also gives an indication as to the strength of the buyers and sellers by their length above and below the body. A long upper shadow indicates an attempt by the buyers to take control but eventually lose out to the sellers. A long lower shadow indicates an attempt by the sellers to take control but eventually lose out to the buyers.

Price charts are calculated and presented in time periods and each point, line, or candle on the chart represents one time period. Table 6.1 is a table of the most common time periods used by binary options platforms.

The term bull in trader's terminology means that the market is rising, therefore a bull candlestick is indicating, for a given time period, a rising currency pair (Figure 6.4).

Table 6.1 Time Periods

Time Period
1 minute
5 minutes
15 minutes
30 minutes
1 hour
4 hours
End of day
End of week
End of month

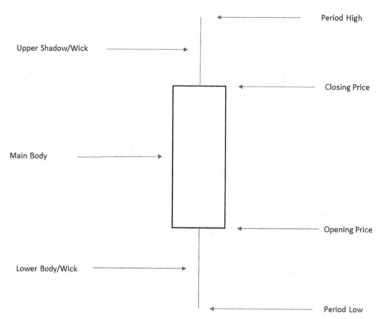

Figure 6.4 Bull candlestick

Similarly, the term bear means that the market is falling and the bear candlestick indicates a falling currency pair for a given time period (Figure 6.5).

What the Single Candlestick Tells You?

As you can see, the candlestick chart offers a more visually pleasing and therefore a simpler interpretation of currency price data than the traditional

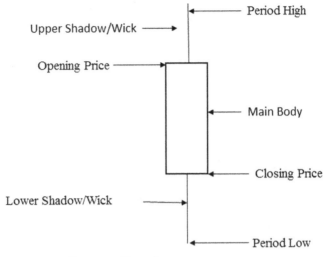

Figure 6.5 Bear candlestick

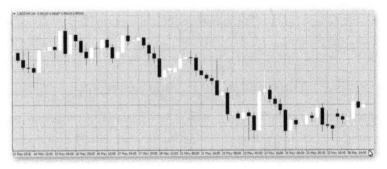

Figure 6.6 USD/CHF 4 hour candlestick chart

bar charts because a single candlestick gives a straightforward decipher-able image of the price action. You are immediately able to compare the relationship between the high and low prices as well as the opening and closing prices. As you can see from Figure 6.6, there are several shapes to a single candlestick and each shape can give you vital information.

A black filled candlestick, which has a full body, a small wick, and hardly a shadow below the main body, indicates a strong bearish trend during a 4-hour-period with a lot of selling pressure.

A white filled candle that has a very short wick and shadow indicates a bullish trend with a lot of buying pressure.

A black or white filled candle with a long wick, very small body, and a short shadow indicates uncertainty in the market as to the direction of the currency pair. This candle indicates strong buying pressure at the beginning of the session before sellers entered the market and pushed the price back down again. Any bullish or bearish partiality is based on the preceding and following price action.

A black or white filled candle that has a very long shadow and a short upper wick with the opening and closing prices being very close together also shows uncertainty in the market. It usually indicates that there was strong selling pressure before buyers eventually entered the market and forced the price up toward the end of the session.

There are numerous other candlestick chart patterns that can be interpreted by a trader to indicate the future direction of the market. For details of these please refer to my book, *Competing in the Financial Markets*. However, binary option trading tends to rely more on strategies that are derived from technical analysis tools, indicators, and trends rather than chart patterns.

Binary Option Trading Strategies

Moving averages are fundamentally a set of data points that represent a number of closing prices over a specific time period. These are joined together by a line drawn on a candlestick price chart. The time periods most commonly used are 1 minute, 5 minutes, 15 minutes, 30 minutes, 60 minutes, 4 hours, daily, weekly, or monthly. The most common number of moving average series of closing prices used is 5, 10, 20, 50, 100, and 200. There are two commonly used moving average types used by traders today.

Simple Moving Average

The simple moving average (SMA) is calculated by adding the number of closing prices for the number of periods chosen and then dividing the total by the number of periods. For example, if we had a 10-period moving average on a 60-minute time frame, the closing prices for the last 10 hours are added together and then divided by 10. The result would become the latest data point and the furthest data point or closing price would be dropped.

Exponential Moving Average

The exponential moving average (EMA) differs from the SMA in that it doesn't drop the first price in a series when the latest price is calculated. If, for example, we have specified a 10 series EMA, the first calculation will be the same as the SMA; however, when the next price in the series becomes available, the calculation will retain the original 10 prices plus the new price to arrive at the new average. The EMA line consequently follows the price action much more closely than the SMA.

Rainbow EMA Strategy

Essentially what an EMA does, is attempt to reduce the muddle and the noise of the everyday price action. The second thing that an EMA does is to smooth the price and to expose the trend and sometimes it can also expose patterns that you couldn't otherwise see. This particular binary options trading strategy is simple to set up and simple to execute. It is called a rainbow moving average strategy because it uses three EMAs, which indicate the optimum time to trade when the three lines fan out like a rainbow.

The setup and rules for this strategy are as follows:

- The three moving averages use time periods of 26, 14, and 6.
- When the 14 and 6 period moving average lines cross above the 26 period moving average line, it indicates a possible up (bull) trending market. Conversely, when the 14 and 6 period moving average lines cross below the 26 moving average line, it indicates a possible down (bear) trending market.
- Only trade when the 6 period moving average is above the 14 period moving average and the 14 period moving average is above the 26 period moving average in an uptrend. The reverse

is true when the market is in a down trend where the 26 period moving average will be above the 14 and 6 period moving averages.

- Prices (candles) must be above the 26 period moving average to buy a call.
- Prices (candles) must be below the 26 period moving average to buy a put.
- A trade should only take place when the three moving average lines are spread out like a fan.
- When the three moving average lines are close together a trade is not a viable strategy.
- The period traded can be 15, 30, or 60 minute time frames.

In Figure 6.7 we shall look at a strategy using a 60-minute time frame. The criteria we shall use also applies to a 15- or 30-minute time frame.

First, as per our rules for this trading strategy where the moving average lines have converged or are converging, we don't trade as no viable or clear trade triggers present themselves. However, once a crossover has occurred, the moving average lines start to fan out. On this chart there is an upward movement with the prices above the 26 period moving average. The strategy is to take advantage of the pullbacks. In other words, as the market moves upwards every now and again, the market pulls back and the prices break the 6 and/or 14 period moving average lines. When this happens this triggers an entry signal to buy a call. There are two pullback moments indicated in Figure 6.7, which both trigger a call buy. The time to expiry of the call should be 30 minutes when using the 1 hour time

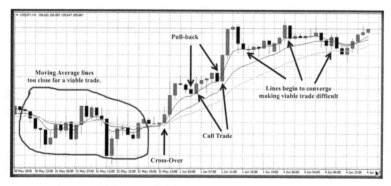

Figure 6.7 USD/JPY 1 hour chart

frame. However, if you were using the 15- or 30-minute time frames, your time to expiry would be 15 and 8 minutes, approximately half of the time frames used. The chart clearly indicates that both binary option trades would have been successful.

EMA 5 Minute Strategy Using 6, 20, and 50 Period EMAs

This strategy is another EMA strategy that uses a crossover in its setup. The first step is to properly set up your chart with the appropriate EMAs so we will be able to identify the EMA cross at the later stage. This EMA strategy uses the 6, 20, and 50 period EMAs.

The second rule for this EMA strategy is the necessity for the price to trade above both 6, 20, and 50 EMAs in the case of a bullish trend, or trade below the 6, 20, and 50 period EMAs in the case of a bearish trend. The third rule is that you need to wait for the EMA crossover, which will add more credence to the bullish or bearish cause.

The EMA crossover for a call is when the 6 and 20 period EMAs cross above the 50 period EMA. Conversely, an EMA crossover for a put is when the 6 and 20 period EMAs cross below the 50 period EMA.

The EMA crossover creates automatic call and put signals. However, since the market is disposed to make a lot of false breakouts, you need more evidence than just a simple EMA crossover to be able to trade successfully. At this stage, we don't know if the bullish sentiment is strong enough to push the price up further after you execute a call, or that the bearish sentiment is strong enough to push the price down after you execute a put.

To avoid the false breakout, you need a fresh convergence to support your view. You need to wait for the prices (bull candle body) to be formed above the 6 period EMA to buy a call or in the case of a downward market wait for the prices (bear candle body) to form below the 6 period moving average before you buy a put. Prices (bull candles or bear candles) that cross the 6 period EMA are not viable trade signals. After the EMA crossover happens, you need to exercise a little patience and wait for the bull or bear candles to form above (bull) or below (bear) the 6 period moving average. Time to expiry of both calls and puts should be 5 minutes maximum.

Figure 6.8 EUR/GBP 5 minute chart

Figure 6.8 indicates that over a period of 5 hours there were eight trading opportunities conforming to the rules of this strategy. If executed, they would have all been successful trades.

Relative Strength Index (RSI) 80/20 Strategy

The RSI indicator is one of the most popular indicators used by traders on many markets including stocks, forex, futures, and binary options. This particular strategy will identify a break in the trend and take advantage of any movement in the other direction.

The default setting for the RSI indicator is a period of 14; however, for this particular strategy we are going to use a period of 8. You can adjust the RSI indicator to your liking on all trading platforms. A period of 8 is far more responsive to the market than the 14 period setting. This is important as we shall be looking at overbought and oversold price areas. In addition, we should change the overbought and oversold lines from 70/30 to 80/20. Once again your platform will facilitate this change. The RSI is the only indicator we shall use for this strategy; the reason being that there are strict rules for deciding on the right moment to trade. Trade moments do not come up regularly with this strategy but when they do, you will have a 90 percent plus success rate.

Using Figure 6.9 we are going to look at the rules for this particular strategy. We are using a 60 minute chart for this example; however, the strategy can be used in any time frame.

Figure 6.9 USD/CAD 60 minute chart

The first step is to find a currency pair where a reversal in the trend looks likely. You can identify a possible reversal by checking the RSI indicator and noting where the signal line is on the indicator. If it is approaching the 20 (oversold area) or the 80 (overbought area) levels then there is the possibility of a potential moment when a trend reversal takes place and you can trade. On the chart above I have indicated two such moments with a white circle. The first moment is a potential call where the downward trend reverses and the second moment a potential put where the upward trend reverses.

Once the RSI line touches or moves below the 20 level (white circle 1) you have a strong potential for a trend reversal from downwards to upwards. Wait for the next candle to start forming. In this case it is a bull candle indicating a reversal from the previous trend. At this point a binary options call trade with the time frame of 60 minutes should be executed. As we can see from the chart such a strategy would have resulted in a successful binary options trade.

Similarly, later on the price (RSI line) moves above the 80 into the over-bought area giving the potential for a reversal in the trend from an uptrend to a downtrend. Once again wait for the next candle to form which in this case is a bear candle and then buy a put option with a time frame of 60 minutes. Such a strategy, as we can see, yielded a successful binary option trade.

Stochastic Oscillator

The Stochastic Oscillator is a very good tool to trade binary options but in order to trade successfully you need to be patient. The settings for the oscillator for this strategy are 14, 3 and 7. Your trading platform will have the oscillator as part of its indicator package and also you will be able to change the settings from the standard numbers to the ones I have indicated. The oscillator gives you exact bull and bear setups, which enable you to buy call and put binary options. The oscillator has two lines, a fast line and a slow line, and when the fast line has crossed above the slow line, it indicates an upward moving market where the prices are increasing. When the fast line crosses below the slow line, it indicates a downward trend where prices are falling. Just like the RSI the stochastic indicates when the market is either overbought (the stochastic is above the 80 level) or oversold (the stochastic is below the 20 level).

This is where you have to show patience. The rules for this strategy are:

1. Don't trade when stochastic is between the overbought and oversold levels.
2. Wait for the fast line to cross from above to below the slow line in the overbought area before buying a put or wait for the fast line to cross from below to above the slow line before buying a call.
3. Wait for the two lines to diverge before buying a call or a put.
4. The ideal time frame to trade is a 5 minutes call or put.

Figure 6.10 shows approximately 5 hours of the price trends in 5 minute candles and the stochastic oscillator tracking the prices. During this period there have been five *moments* when the fast line has crossed

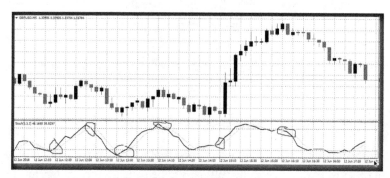

Figure 6.10 GBP/USD 5 minute chart

the slow line and diverged. These instances are shown in the white circles. Note that you must wait to see what sort of candle is forming before buying a call (bull candle) or buying a put (bear candle). As you can see from the chart, five out of the six trades would have been successful. The fourth circle from the left is a potential successful put buy as long as you showed patience and waited for the appropriate bear candle to form. If you jumped in too soon you would have had a losing trade.

The four binary option strategies outlined above are my personal favorites and I have enjoyed much success trading them. If you follow the rules I have laid out you too will enjoy a lot of success employing these strategies.

CHAPTER 7

Option Strangle and Straddle Strategies

As we have discussed earlier, options fill the requirement to have a trading strategy with limited loss and unlimited profit potential. There are a number of options strategies that traders across the globe use. In this chapter we will discuss the straddle and strangle strategy in options.

Long Straddle

The long straddle option strategy is used when you expect big movements in the price of the underlying asset but are unsure as to the exact direction of the price movement. To execute a long straddle you buy a call and a put with identical strike prices and identical expiry times. With this strategy, as long as the price at expiry is far enough away to ensure a profit on one of the options that is larger than the combined premiums of the options, the combined options will be in the money at expiry (see Figure 7.1).

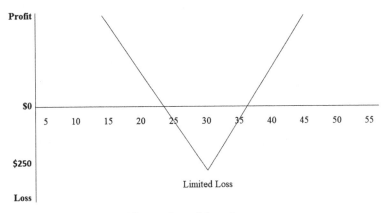

Figure 7.1 Long straddle profit and loss diagram

The profit and loss diagram for the long straddle shows that both put and call options have the same strike price and the same expiry date. Whichever direction the stock price moved, as long as it moved far enough to cover the combined premiums paid, one of the options would be in the money. Let's see how this works.

A stock is currently trading at $30 a share. As we explained earlier, for the straddle option strategy you would enter into two option positions, one call and one put. The call is for a strike price of $30 and costs $100 ($1 per option × 100 shares) and the put is for a strike price of $30 and costs $150 ($1.50 per option × 100 shares). If the price of the stock stays between $28.50 and $31 over the life of the option (break-even price for the call is $31 and for the put is $28.50), your loss will be $250 (total cost of the two option contracts). You will start to make money once the price of the stock starts to move outside of the range.

Table 7.1 details the calculations of this straddle strategy.

Suppose that the price of the stock ends up at $45. You would allow the put option to expire worthless and your loss on the put will be $150. The call option, however, has gained substantially and is worth $1,500. After deducting the premiums you paid for the call and the put, your total profit would be $1,250.

Table 7.1a shows the profit and loss profile for a long straddle strategy for a range of expiry prices. In particular it shows maximum possible

Table 7.1 Long straddle option contract stock trade example

Option	Expires	Strike price	Premium	Total premium	Price at expiry	Action at expiry	Profit/loss
Call	1 month	$30	$1	100 × $1 = $100	$45	Exercise	($45 − $30) × 100 − ($100 + $150) = $1,250
Put	1 month	$30	$1.5	100 × $1.5 = $150	$45	Expire	−$150

Table 7.1a *Long straddle stock option strategy*

Stock price at expiration	Long 30 call profit/(loss) at expiration	Long 30 put profit/(loss) at expiration	Long straddle profit/(loss) at expiration
34	3	(1.5)	1.5
33	2	(1.5)	0.5
32	1	(1.5)	(0.5)
31	0	(1.5)	(1.5)
30	(1)	(1.5)	(2.5)
29	(1)	(0.5)	(1.5)
28	(1)	0.5	(0.5)
27	(1)	1.5	0.5
26	(1)	2.5	1.5
25	(1)	3.5	2.5
24	(1)	4.5	3.5

profit and maximum possible loss for a long call strike price of 30 and a long put strike price of 30. Recall that 1 index option contract has a multiplier of 100, therefore the numbers in Table 7.1a should be multiplied by 100 to calculate actual profit or loss of the long strangle strategy. This strategy can also be used for stock index and currency options equally as well.

Short Straddle

The short straddle strategy is very risky as there is no scope for the price at all beyond the value of the option premiums. As you can see from the diagram in Figure 7.2, the price of the stock has to remain in a small band for the writer of this straddle to have any chance of making a profit.

The straddle option buyer would let both options expire worthless if at the expiry date the stock price was within the $28.50 to $31 price band. The best strategy for a short straddle writer is to not write options on stocks but look for a currency pair that is ranging between strong resistance and support prices with enough room for the price to make a normal daily range.

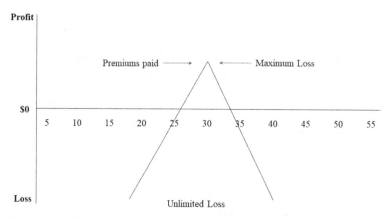

Figure 7.2 Short straddle profit and loss diagram

Table 7.2 Short straddle option contract currency trade example

Option	Expires	Strike price	Premium	Total premium	Price at expiry	Action at expiry	Profit/ loss
Call	1 month	1.1750	0.0040	$400	$116.5	Expire	$400
Put	1 month	1.1680	0.0035	$350	$116.5	Expire	$350

The most one can begin to try to profit from these kinds of strategies would be to look for a currency pair where there is strong resistance overhead and strong resistance below, and enough room in between for the price to make a normal daily range; see Table 7.2. Bear in mind that currency option contracts are 100 options per lot and 1,000 units of base currency. Therefore, the writer of the short straddle receives (0.0040 × 100 × 1000 = $400) premium on the call and (00.35 × 100 × 1,000 = $350 on the put. Giving the option writer $750 profit. A short straddle with the strike prices just beyond the support and resistance levels could end with a nice profit because the buyer of the options would allow both to expire worthless as they are both out of the money.

Table 7.2a shows the profit and loss profile for a currency short straddle strategy for a range of expiry prices. In particular it shows maximum possible profit and maximum possible loss for a short call strike price of 1.1750 and a short put strike price of 1.1680. Remember that a currency options contract has a multiplier of 100 and each contract is 1,000 units of

Table 7.2a Currency short straddle strategy

Currency price at expiration	Short 1.1750 call profit/ (loss) at expiration	Short 1.1680 put profit/(loss) at expiration	Short straddle profit/(loss) at expiration
1.1780	0.0010	(0.0065)	(0.0055)
1.1770	0.0020	(0.0055)	(0.0035)
1.1760	0.0030	(0.0045)	(0.0015)
1.1750	0.0040	(0.0035)	0.0005
1.1740	0.0040	(0.0025)	0.0015
1.1730	0.0040	(0.0015)	0.0025
1.1720	0.0040	(0.0005)	0.0035
1.1710	0.0040	0.0005	0.0045
1.1700	0.0040	0.0015	0.0055
1.1690	0.0040	0.0025	0.0065
1.1680	0.0040	0.0035	0.0075
1.1670	0.0040	0.0035	0.0075
1.1660	0.0040	0.0035	0.0075
1.1650	0.0040	0.0035	0.0075
1.1640	0.0040	0.0035	0.0075

base currency; therefore, the numbers in Table 7.2a should be multiplied by 100,000 to calculate actual profit or loss of the short straddle strategy. This strategy can also be used for stock and index options equally as well.

Long Strangle

A long strangle option strategy is a strategy to use when you expect a price movement, but are not sure in which direction the move will go. To execute this strategy, you should buy both call and put options, with different strike prices but with identical expiry times. Exactly which strike prices you buy the options at depends on what expectations you have of the future price. For example, if you think a breakout from the current range with an increase in price is more likely, you can make the strike price of the call option relatively low and the strike price of the put option relatively high. Remember, the most you can lose is the combined price of the two options, whereas your profit potential is, at least hypothetically, unlimited.

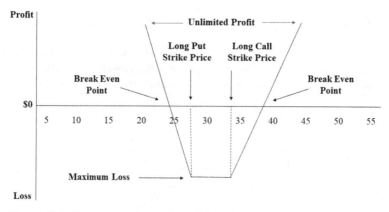

Figure 7.3 Long strangle profit and loss diagram

Figure 7.3 clearly shows that the strike prices of the two options reflect the buyers' expectations for the future price movement of the underlying stock. The strike price for the call is $34 and the strike price of the put is $27, and the price of the stock is $31. The premium paid on the call is $1 and the put is $1.5. Once the price moves beyond the break-even price of $35 for the call, the option is deemed in the money and the buyer will be looking to exercise it at expiry. The put option would be deemed in the money once the stock price had fallen below the break-even price for the put of $25.50. If the price at expiry was $45, the long strangle buyer would exercise the call and allow the put to expire worthless. Table 7.3 shows the mathematics of the long strangle trade.

As you can observe, the long strangle buyer would make a profit of $550 if the stock price is at $45 at the expiry date, which is the profit on the call option minus both premiums paid. The strangle option buyer would allow both the call and put options to expire worthless if the stock price stayed in the range of $27 to $35. In this case the total loss for the option buyer would be the cost ($250) of the two premiums paid to the option writer.

Table 7.3a shows the profit and loss profile for a long strangle strategy for a range of expiry prices. In particular it shows maximum possible profit and maximum possible loss for a long call strike price of 30 and a long put strike price of 27. Remember that 1 index option contract has a multiplier of 100, therefore the numbers in Table 7.3a should be

Table 7.3 Long strangle option contract stock trade example

Option	Expires	Strike price	Premium	Total premium	Price at expiry	Action at expiry	Profit/loss
Call	1 month	$34	$1	100 × $1 = $100	$45	Exercise	($45 − $34) × 100 − ($100 + $150) =$850
Put	1 month	$27	$1.5	100 × $1.5 = $150	$45	Expire	−$150

Table 7.3a Long strangle option contract stock profit and loss

Stock price at expiration	Long 34 call profit/(loss) at expiration	Long 27 put profit/(loss) at expiration	Long strangle profit/(loss) at expiration
45	10	(1.5)	8.5
43	8	(1.5)	6.5
41	6	(1.5)	4.5
39	4	(1.5)	2.5
37	2	(1.5)	(0.5)
35	0	(1.5)	(1.5)
33	(1)	(1.5)	(2.5)
31	(1)	(1.5)	(2.5)
29	(1)	(1.5)	(2.5)
27	(1)	(1.5)	(2.5)
25	(1)	1	0

multiplied by 100 to calculate actual profit or loss of the long strangle strategy. This strategy can also be used for stock index and currency options equally as well.

Short Strangle

The short strangle is an options position from the point of view of the option writer. It is the exact opposite of a long strangle. It is a slight adjustment to the short straddle and attempts to improve the success of the trade for the writer of the options by widening the break-even points. Which means that there needs to be much greater movement in the underlying asset to enable the call and put options to be worth exercising (Figure 7.4).

This strategy comprises the concurrent selling (writing) of a touch out of the money (OTM) put and a slightly out of the money call of the same underlying stock, index or currency, both with the same expiration date. This characteristically means that since the OTM call and put are sold, the net credit received by the writer (seller) is less compared to a short straddle, but the break-even points are also wider. The underlying asset has to move significantly for the call and the put to be worth exercising. If the underlying asset does not show much of a movement, the seller of the short strangle options keep the premiums.

In the example presented in Table 7.4, the investor believes that ABC stock index will hardly move at all over the next month and decides to sell (write) a short strangle.

Suppose ABC stock index is trading at 400 in June. The investor executes a short strangle by selling a July 390 OTM put for $10 and a July 450 OTM call for $11. The net premium received to enter the trade is $21, which is also the investors maximum possible profit.

If ABC stock index rallies and is trading at 500 on expiration in July, the July 390 put will expire worthless but the July 450 call expires in the money and has an intrinsic value of $50,000. Remember that usually the multiplier is 100, therefore if the index is at the 500 level the value

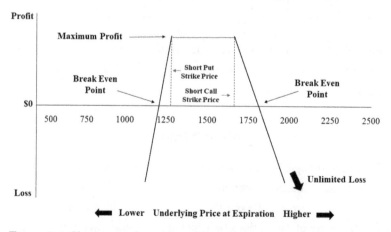

Figure 7.4 Short strangle profit and loss diagram

Table 7.4 Short strangle options strategy index trade example

Option	Expires	Strike price	Premium	Total premium	Price at expiry	Action at expiry	Profit/loss
Call	July	450	$11	100 × $11 = $1,100	400	Expire	$1,100
Put	July	390	$10	100 × $10 = $1,000	400	Expire	$1,000

Table 7.4a Short strangle index profit and loss

Index price at expiration	Short 450 call profit/(loss) at expiration	Short 390 put profit/(loss) at expiration	Short strangle profit/(loss) at expiration
520	(59)	10	(49)
500	(39)	10	(29)
480	(19)	10	(9)
460	1	10	11
440	11	10	21
420	11	10	21
400	11	10	21
380	11	0	11
360	11	(20)	(9)
340	11	(40)	(29)
320	11	(60)	(49)

is 500 − 450 × (100 × 50) = $5,000. Subtracting the initial received premium of $2,100 (21 × 100), the investors loss comes to $2,900.

However, if on expiration in July the ABC stock index is still trading at 400, both the July 390 put and the July 450 call expire worthless and the investor gets to keep the entire initial premium of $2,100 received to enter the trade as profit.

The risk associated with this strategy is unlimited if the stock index moves a long way from any of the two break-even points, which are 380 for the put and 461 for the call. As long as the stock index level stays between the 380 and 461 level, neither option will be exercised and both will be allowed to expire worthless.

Table 7.4a shows the profit and loss profile for a short strangle strategy for a range of expiry prices. In particular it shows maximum possible profit and maximum possible loss for a short call strike price of 450 and a short put strike price of 390. Notice that a price at expiration between the two strike prices offers the most profit from this strategy. Remember that 1 index options contract has a multiplier of 100, therefore the numbers in Table 7.4a should be multiplied by 100 to calculate actual profit or loss of the short strangle strategy.

This strategy can also be used for stock and currency options equally as well.

CHAPTER 8

Bullish Strategies

Bullish strategies in options trading are used when the investor expects the underlying asset price to move upwards. It is necessary to assess how high the asset price can go and the time frame in which the rally will occur in order to select the optimal trading strategy.

The most bullish strategies are the simplest ones where the investor executes a plain vanilla call option. These strategies are the ones that you would probably try out as a newbie options trader. However, call options have a limited life span. If the underlying stock price does not move above the strike price before the option expiration date, the call option will expire worthless.

Assume that it is May and you believe that the price (currently $160) of ABC shares will appreciate over the next months. To take advantage of this you decide to buy one lot (100 call option contracts) at the money and at the price of $2.02 each with an expiration in July. The price is the premium paid. You have effectively bought the right but not the obligation to buy 100 ABC shares before or on the 18th July. For this right you have paid a premium of just $202 instead of paying $16,000 for the 100 shares. If the price of ABC shares on the 18th July is $152 (out of the money) you let the option expire worthless and your loss is the premium paid. However, if before or on the 18th July the price of ABC shares has increased in value to say $170 per share (in the money), you could exercise the option at the strike price of $160 per share giving you a profit of $100 \times (\$170 - \$160) = \$1,000$ less the premium you paid of $202, leaving you with a profit of $798 on the trade.

Table 8.1 is an example of an option strategy exercised in the money on or before the expiration date (Figure 8.1).

Table 8.1 ABC stock option trade exercised (in the money)

Stock	Strike price	Expiry date	Call/ put	Price at expiry	Premium	Contracts	Profit
ABC	$160	18th July	Call	$170	$2.02	100	$798

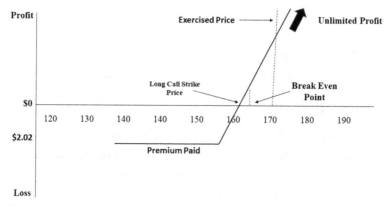

Figure 8.1 ABC stock long call strategy

Table 8.2 ABC stock option trade (out of the money)

Stock	Strike price	Contracts	Expiry date	Call/ put	Premium	Price at expiry	Loss
ABC	$160	100	18th July	Call	$2.02	−$8	$202

Table 8.2 provides an example of the same option strategy expiring out of the money with just the loss of the premium to the option holder.

The strategy in this example is a purchase of call options. But what if you were a writer of an option and not the purchaser? As a writer who was bullish on ABC stock, your strategy would be to sell a put and receive the premium. You would be hoping that the put option would be allowed to expire worthless by the buyer of the put because the stock price was out of the money at the expiration date and had risen to a level above the break-even price. Thus you could pocket the premium and that would be your profit. However, your risk would be that the stock price falls and is exercised in the money leaving you with a bigger loss than the premium you collected.

Table 8.3 Option strategy

Option type	Strategy
Long call	Bullish
Long put	Bearish
Short put	Bullish
Short call	Bearish

As we mentioned earlier in this book, it is worth bearing in mind that there are four positions that you can take depending on your options strategy and whether you are bullish or bearish on a particular asset (Table 8.3).

The long call strategy is the most bullish but riskiest of all the bullish strategies and should only be used when all technical and fundamental indicators are indicating that the underlying asset is on the rise. This strategy can also be used for stock index and currency options equally as well.

A more conservative or moderate bullish strategy is the bull call spread option which is used when the investor believes that the price of the underlying asset will increase moderately in the short term.

Bull Call Spread Strategy

Bull call spreads can be executed by buying an at the money call option (long call) while at the same time writing (short call) a higher striking out of the money call option of the same underlying security and the same expiration month. By shorting the out of the money call option you would reduce the cost of establishing the bullish position. On the other hand you would forgo the chance of making a large profit if the underlying asset price rises steeply (Figure 8.2).

Maximum profit is gained for the bull call spread options strategy when the stock price moves above the higher strike price of the two calls and it is equal to the difference between the strike price of the two call options minus the initial net premium given to enter the position.

The formula for working out the maximum profit is:

- Strike Price of Short Call − Strike Price of Long Call − Net Premium Paid = Maximum Profit
- Maximum profit reached when underlying asset $>=$ Strike Price of Short Call

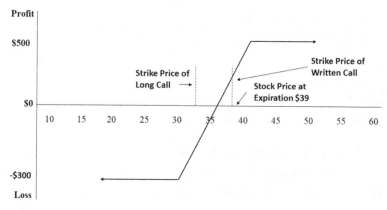

Figure 8.2 XYZ stock bull call spread strategy

The bull call spread strategy will culminate in a loss if the stock price declines at expiration. However, the maximum loss cannot be more than the initial net premium given to enter the spread position.

The formula for achieving maximum loss is:

- Maximum loss = Net Premium Paid
- Maximum loss happens when price of underlying asset ≤ Strike Price of Long Call

Let's look at a practical example. It is June and you believe that XYZ stock, which is trading at $35, is going to rally soon and you enter a bull call spread by buying a July 33 call for $4 and writing a July 38 call for $1. The net investment required to put on the bull spread is a net premium given of $3.

The stock price of XYZ begins to rise and closes at $39 on expiration date. Both options expire in the money with the July 33 call having a value of $2 ($6 increase in stock price − $4 cost of long call) and the July 38 call having a value of $0 (premium received − $1 increase in stock price). This means that the option spread is now worth $3 at expiration.

If the price of XYZ had declined to 30 instead, both options would expire worthless. You would lose your entire investment of $3 per share, which is also your maximum possible loss.

Table 8.4 shows the profit and loss profile for a bull call spread for a range of expiry prices. In particular it shows maximum possible profit and maximum possible loss for a long call strike price of 33 and a short call strike price of 38. Remember that 1 option stock contract is 100 shares,

Table 8.4 *XYZ stock bull call spread profit and loss*

Stock price at expiration	Long 33 call profit/(loss) at expiration	Short 38 call profit/(loss) at expiration	Bull call spread profit/(loss) at expiration
41	4	(2)	2
40	3	(1)	2
39	2	0	2
38	1	1	2
37	0	1	1
36	(1)	1	0
35	(2)	1	(1)
34	(3)	1	(2)
33	(4)	1	(3)
32	(4)	1	(3)
31	(4)	1	(3)
30	(4)	1	(3)

therefore the numbers in Table 8.4 should be multiplied by 100 to calculate actual profit or loss of the bull call spread. This strategy can also be used for stock index and currency options equally as well.

Bull Put Spread Strategy

The bull put spread option trading strategy is used when the options trader believes that the price of the underlying asset will move up moderately in the short term. The bull put spread options strategy is also known as the bull put credit spread as the difference between the premium paid and the premium received is credit balance when executing the trade. Bull put spreads are executed by selling (writing) a higher strike price in the money put option and buying a lower strike price out of the money put option on the same underlying stock with exactly the same expiration date.

Both options will expire worthless if the stock price closes above the higher strike price on expiration date and the bull put spread option strategy earns the maximum profit, which is equal to the net premium received when entering the position.

The formula for calculating maximum profit is:

- Maximum Profit = Net Premium Received
- Maximum Profit Achieved When Price of Underlying >= Strike Price of Short Put

If the stock price falls below the lower strike price on expiration date, then the bull put spread strategy suffers a maximum loss equal to the difference between the strike prices of the two puts minus the net premium received when executing on the trade.

The formula for calculating maximum loss is:

- Maximum Loss = Strike Price of Short Put − Strike Price of Long Put − Net Premium Received
- Maximum Loss Occurs When Price of Underlying ≤ Strike Price of Long Put

The underlying price at which break-even is realized for the bull put spread position is calculated by means of the following formula.

- Break-even Point = Strike Price of Short Put − Net Premium Received

Let's look at a practical example of opening a bull put spread position. Assume it is March and you believe that XYZ stock trading at $39 is going to rally in the near term and you decide to enter a bull put spread by buying a May 36 put for $1 and writing (selling) a May 45 put for $3. You receive the difference between the premium paid and the premium received of $2 when you enter the bull put position.

The stock price of XYZ begins to rise and closes at $42 on expiration date. Both options expire worthless and you keep the entire premium credit of $2. This is the maximum profit possible.

If the price of XYZ had fallen to $34 instead, both the May 36 long put and the May 45 short put would expire in the money and have a value of $1 and ($8), respectively. This means that the spread is now worth ($7) on expiration. This is your maximum possible loss for this bull put spread.

Table 8.5 shows the profit and loss profile for a bull put spread for a range of expiry prices. In particular it shows maximum possible profit and maximum possible loss for a long put strike price of 36 and a short put strike price of 45. Recall that 1 option stock contract is 100 shares, therefore the numbers in Table 8.5 should be multiplied by 100 to calculate actual profit or loss of the bull put spread (Figure 8.3).

This strategy can also be used for stock index and currency options equally as well.

Table 8.5 XYZ stock bull put spread profit and loss

Stock price at expiration	Long 36 put profit/(loss) at expiration	Short 45 put profit/(loss) at expiration	Bull put spread profit/(loss) at expiration
47	(1)	3	2
46	(1)	3	2
45	(1)	3	2
44	(1)	2	1
43	(1)	1	0
42	(1)	0	(1)
41	(1)	(1)	(2)
40	(1)	(2)	(3)
39	(1)	(3)	(4)
38	(1)	(4)	(5)
37	(1)	(5)	(6)
36	(1)	(6)	(7)
35	0	(7)	(7)
34	1	(8)	(7)
33	2	(9)	(7)
32	3	(10)	(7)
31	4	(11)	(7)

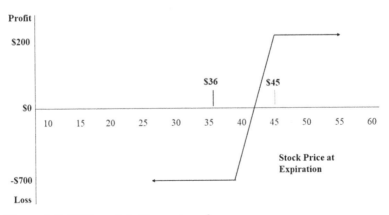

Figure 8.3 XYZ stock bull put spread strategy

CHAPTER 9

Bearish Strategies

Bearish option strategies are used when the options investor believes the underlying stock price is going to move downwards. It is essential the investor assesses how low the stock price can fall and the time frame in which the decline will occur in order to select the best trading strategy.

The most bearish of options strategies is the simple put option buying strategy. This is a strategy that is used by most newbie investors just like you and is utilized when the stock price is expected to move quite a bit from current price.

It is unusual for a stock price to make steep movements either up or down. So when investors believe the share price will have a moderate move downwards, they use bear spreads to reduce their risk. While their maximum profit is capped for these strategies, they more often than not cost less to employ.

Long Put Options Strategy

The long put option strategy is a straightforward strategy in options trading where the investor buys put options with the belief that the price of the underlying security will move significantly below the strike price before the expiration date is reached. However, put options have a restricted life span. If the underlying assets price does not move below the strike price before the options expiration date, the put option will expire worthless.

Since in theory a stock price can reach zero at expiration date (a much less realistic expectation for an index or a currency), the maximum profit possible when using the long put strategy is only limited to the strike price of the purchased put less the price paid for the option.

The formula for calculating profit is:

- Maximum Profit Achieved When Underlying Price = 0
- Profit = Strike Price of Long Put – Premium Paid

The risk for executing a long put strategy is limited to the price paid for the put option, however high the underlying price is trading on expiration date (Figure 9.1).

The formula for calculating maximum loss is:

- Maximum Loss = Premium Paid
- Maximum Loss Occurs When Price of Underlying ≥ Strike Price of Long Put

The underlying asset price at which break-even is achieved for the long put position is:

- Strike Price of Long Put – Premium Paid = Break-Even Price

Now let's assume that it's October and you believe that the price of XYZ stock will decline sharply in the next couple of months. The current price is $140. You decide to execute a November put option contract with a strike price of $140 priced at $6.50. You have effectively bought the right but not

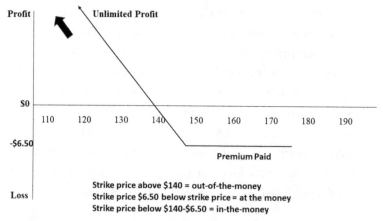

Figure 9.1 XYZ long put strategy

the obligation to sell 100 shares (1 option contract = 100 shares) before or on the November expiration date. For this right you have paid a premium of just $6.50 instead of paying $14,000 for the 100 shares. Suppose you were proven right and the price of XYZ stock falls to $130 at option expiration date. With the underlying stock price at $130, your put option will now be in the money with an intrinsic value of $130. Since you had paid $6.50 to purchase the put option, your net profit for the entire trade is $3.50.

However, if you were wrong in your assessment and the stock price had instead rallied to $150, you let your put option expire worthless giving you a loss of the $6.50 that you paid to purchase the option.

Table 9.1 is an example of an option strategy exercised in the money on or before the expiration date.

Table 9.2 is an example of the same option strategy expiring out of the money with just the loss of the premium to the option holder.

The strategy in this example is a purchase of put options. But what if you were a writer of an option and not the purchaser? As a writer who was bearish on XYZ stock, your strategy would be to sell a call and receive the premium. You would be hoping that the call option would be allowed to expire worthless by the buyer of the call because the stock price was out of the money at the expiration date and had fallen to a level below the break-even price. Thus you could pocket the premium and that would be your profit. However, your risk would be that the stock price rises and is exercised in the money leaving you with a bigger loss than the premium you collected.

Table 9.1 XYZ stock option trade exercised (in the money)

Stock	Strike price	Expiry	Call/ put	Price at expiry	Premium	Shares	Profit
XYZ	$140	November	Put	$130	$6.50	100	$3,500

Table 9.2 XYZ stock option trade (out of the money)

Stock	Strike price	Expiry	Call/ put	Price at expiry	Premium	Shares	Loss
XYZ	$140	November	Put	$150	6.50	100	$6.50

Table 9.3 XYZ long put strategy profit and loss

Stock price at expiration	Long 140 put profit/(loss) at expiration
150	(6.50)
148	(6.50)
146	(6.50)
144	(6.50)
142	(6.50)
140	(6.50)
138	(4.50)
136	(2.50)
134	(0.50)
132	1.50
130	3.50
128	5.50

The long put strategy is the most bearish but riskiest of all the bearish strategies and as with the long call strategy, should only be used when all technical and fundamental indicators are indicating that the underlying asset is going to decline. This strategy can also be used for stock index and currency options equally as well (Table 9.3).

A more conservative or moderate bearish strategy is the bear call spread option, which is used when the investor believes that the price of the underlying asset will decrease moderately in the short term.

Bear Call Spread

This option strategy is also known as the bear call credit spread as a credit (premium) is received upon executing the trade. The spread is made up of 1 out of the money long call and 1 in the money short call. They can be executed by buying call options at a certain strike price and selling the same number of call options at a lower strike price on the same underlying asset expiring in the same month.

The maximum profit possible using the bear call spread options strategy is the credit premium received upon executing the trade. To attain the maximum profit, the stock price needs to close below the strike price of the short call at expiration date when both options would expire worthless.

Maximum profit is:

- Maximum Profit = Net Premium Received
- Maximum Profit Realized When Price of Underlying <= Strike Price of Short Call

If the stock price moves above the strike price of the long call at the expiration date, then the bear call spread strategy suffers a maximum loss equal to the difference in strike price between the two options minus the original net premium received when opening the position.

Maximum loss is:

- Maximum Loss = Strike Price of Long Call − Strike Price of Short Call − Net Premium Received
- Maximum Loss Arises When Price of Underlying >= Strike Price of Long Call

The underlying price at which break-even point is achieved for the bear call spread position is the strike price of the short call plus the net premium received (Figure 9.2).

Let's look at a practical example of the Bear Call Strategy. You are bearish on XYZ stock, which is trading at $39 in June. You decide to enter into a bear call spread position by buying a July 42 call for $1 and

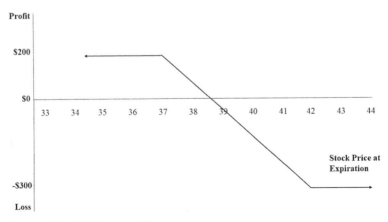

Figure 9.2 XYZ bear call strategy

selling a July 37 call for $3 at the same time, giving you a net $2 net premium for executing this trade.

If on expiration the price of XYZ stock has dropped to $36, both options would expire worthless, so you get to keep the entire net premium of $2 as profit.

However, if the stock had climbed to $44 instead, both calls will expire in the money with the July 42 long call having $2 in value and the July 37 short call having $7 in value. The spread would then have a net value of $5 (the difference in strike price, $42 – $37). Since you have to buy back the spread for $5, this means you will suffer a net loss of $3 after deducting the $2 credit you earned when you entered the spread position.

Table 9.4 shows the Bear Call Spread's profit and loss for a range of strike prices. It shows that the maximum total loss is $3 and the maximum total gain is $2. Remember that as one option contract is for 100 shares

Table 9.4 XYZ bear call spread strategy profit and loss

Stock price at expiration	Long 42 call profit/(loss) at expiration	Short 37 call profit/(loss) at expiration	Bear call spread profit/(loss) at expiration
47	4	(7)	(3)
46	3	(6)	(3)
45	2	(5)	(3)
44	1	(4)	(3)
43	0	(3)	(3)
42	(1)	(2)	(3)
41	(1)	(1)	(2)
40	(1)	0	(1)
39	(1)	1	0
38	(1)	2	1
37	(1)	3	2
36	(1)	3	2
35	(1)	3	2
34	(1)	3	2
33	(1)	3	2
32	(1)	3	2
31	(1)	3	2

the numbers in Table 9.4 should be multiplied by 100 to come to the actual cost of this bear spread.

If you wanted to execute a more aggressive bear spread position, you would do this by widening the difference between the strike price of the two call options. A word of warning though as this will also mean that the stock price must move further downwards for you to gain the maximum profit. Bear Call Spread can also be employed for index and currency options.

Bear Put Spread Strategy

The bear put spread option trading strategy's usage is similar to that of the bear call spread strategy in that it is used when the investor thinks that the price of the underlying asset will go down moderately in the near term.

Bear put spreads are employed by buying a higher striking in the money long put option and selling a lower striking out of the money short put option of the same underlying security with the same expiration date. A bear put spread is established for a net premium cost (you pay more premium than you receive) and earns as the underlying stock declines in price. Profit is limited if the stock price falls below the strike price of the short put, which is the lower strike price of the two puts, and potential loss is limited if the stock price moves above the strike price of the long put (higher strike).

To attain maximum profit, the stock price needs to close below the strike price of the out of the money put on the expiration date. In this scenario both options expire in the money and the higher strike (long) put that was purchased will have higher intrinsic value than the lower strike (short) put that was sold. Thus, maximum profit for the bear put spread option strategy is equal to the difference in strike prices minus the net premium paid when the position was executed.

Maximum profit is:

- Maximum Profit = Strike Price of Long Put – Strike Price of Short Put – Net Premium Paid
- Maximum Profit Achieved When Price of Underlying $<=$ Strike Price of Short Put

If the stock price rises above the in the money put option strike price at expiration date, then the bear put spread strategy experiences a maximum loss equal to the net premium paid when opening the trade.

Maximum loss is:

- Maximum Loss = Net Premium Paid
- Maximum Loss Occurs When Price of Underlying >= Strike Price of Long Put

The underlying price at which break-even is attained for the bear put spread position is the strike price of the long put minus the net premium paid.

Let's now look at a practical example. Suppose that XYZ stock is trading at $39 in May and you are bearish on the stock. You decide to enter a bear put spread position by buying a June 41 put for $3 and sell a June 36 put for $1 at the same time, resulting in a net premium paid of $200 for executing this position.

The price of XYZ stock drops to $35 at expiration. Both puts expire in the money with the June 41 long call having $6 in intrinsic value and the June 36 short call having $1 in intrinsic value. The spread at that point has a net value of $5 (the difference in strike price). When you deduct the net premium paid when you placed the trade, your net profit is $3. This is also your maximum possible profit.

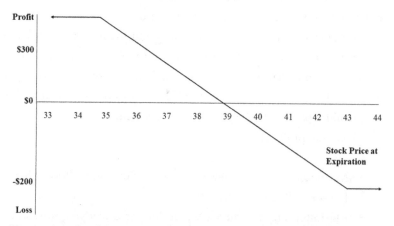

Figure 9.3 Stock bear put spread option strategy

Table 9.5 *XYZ bear put spread strategy profit and loss*

Stock price at expiration	Long 41 put profit/(loss) at expiration	Short 36 put profit/(loss) at expiration	Bear put spread profit/(loss) at expiration
47	(3)	1	(2)
46	(3)	1	(2)
45	(3)	1	(2)
44	(3)	1	(2)
43	(3)	1	(2)
42	(3)	1	(2)
41	(3)	1	(2)
40	(2)	1	(1)
39	(1)	1	0
38	0	1	1
37	1	1	2
36	2	1	3
35	3	0	3
34	4	(1)	3
33	5	(2)	3
32	6	(3)	3
31	7	(4)	3

If the stock had rallied to $43 instead, both options would have expired worthless and you would lose the entire net premium paid of $2 to enter the trade. This is also the maximum possible loss.

Table 9.5 shows the Bear Put Spread's profit and loss for a range of strike prices. It shows that the maximum total loss is $2 and the maximum total gain is $3. Remember that as one option contract is for 100 shares the numbers above should be multiplied by 100 to come to the actual cost of this bear spread.

If you wanted to execute a more aggressive bear spread position, you would do this by widening the difference between the strike price of the two put options. A word of warning though as this will also mean that the stock price must move further downwards for you to gain the maximum profit. Bear put spreads can also be employed for index and currency options strategies.

CHAPTER 10

Hedging Using Options

So far we have been looking at options from the perspective of an investor speculating on the price of an underlying asset. You can think of speculation as gambling on the movement of a financial asset. The big advantage of options is that you aren't restricted to making a profit just when the market moves higher. Because of the adaptability of options, you can also make money when the market moves down or even sideways. To be frank, the odds on a successful speculation are against you because not only do you have to predict whether the asset will move up or down, you also have to predict the time frame in which this will happen and also how much the price will change.

If it's so difficult, why do investors speculate using options? The answer is leverage. You are controlling 100 shares on each stock option contract you enter into and you have similar multiples for index and currency options too. With leverage it only needs a small price change to make big profits. The other main purpose of options is hedging. Think of this as an insurance policy; just like you insure your house or car, options can be used to insure your investments against a downturn.

Let's say it is March and you have a long position of 300 shares in XYZ company. You are concerned that the XYZ shares will depreciate between now and May. You then have several choices.

- You could do nothing and take a chance that shares will not depreciate
- You could sell your share position and potentially miss out on bigger profits
- You could hedge your long share position by purchasing a long put.

You would probably choose, as most prudent investors would, to hedge your dollar long position.

Assuming that the share price is currently $120, you could purchase 3 long put option contracts (each option is equivalent of 100 shares) with a strike price of $120 and pay a premium for the right to sell your long position on expiry in May. If the XYZ share price moves to $130 by the end of May you will let the put options expire worthless (out of the money) and lose the premium paid. However, if as you suspected the XYZ share price deteriorated and fell to $100, you would then exercise your options (in the money) The loss on your long share position would be offset by the profit you made on the put options of $20 profit × 100 shares × 3 contracts, which equals $6,000 less the premium you paid to enter the contract.

It is not a perfect hedge because you lose the premium you paid at the inception of the long put position; however, your loss on the share position if it had fallen to $100 would have been $6,000.

Long put options are also used for hedging long currency and indices positions and because of their flexibility are the ideal hedging instrument for investors of these assets.

CHAPTER 11

Conclusion

I hope this book has given you some understanding of the world of options. Once again, I must stress that options aren't for all investors. Options are sophisticated trading tools that can be risky if you don't educate yourself, as you have done by reading this book, before using them.

A brief summary of what we have covered in this book is as follows:

- An option is a contract giving the buyer the right but not the obligation to buy or sell an underlying asset at a specific price on or before a specific date.
- Options are called derivatives because they derive their value from an underlying asset.
- A call gives the holder the right to buy an asset at a certain price on or before a specific date.
- A put gives the holder the right to sell an asset at a certain price on or before a specific date.
- There are four types of participants in options markets: buyers of calls, sellers of calls, buyers of puts, and sellers of puts.
- Buyers are also referred to as holders and sellers are also referred to as writers.
- The strike price is the price at which an underlying stock can be purchased or sold.
- The total cost of an option is called the premium.
- The premium of an option increases as the chances of the event of the option finishing in the money increases.
- A stock option contract typically represents 100 shares of the underlying stock.
- A currency option typically represents 1,000 units of base currency.

- An index option typically has a contract multiplier of $100.
- Investors use options to speculate and hedge risk.
- The two main classifications of options are American and European.
- Options can also be distinguished as listed/over the counter, or vanilla/exotic.

Please use this book as it was envisioned—to learn more about options and option strategies. They are trading tools that newbie investors and traders like yourselves should master and use wisely and prudently. I hope you have enjoyed and profited from the journey we have just completed and wish you a successful career in option investment and trading.

About the Author

Educated in the United Kingdom, **Philip Cooper** joined Citibank London before moving to Athens as a foreign exchange trader. He was then posted to Citibank's MENA Training Centre in Beirut as the operations manager and a foreign exchange trainer. Returning to the United Kingdom, he joined Union Bank of Switzerland (UBS) as head of learning and development where he trained prospective traders for the trading desk. Later he was appointed head of learning and education for UBS in North America, specifically to develop trading simulations. He later left the bank to create a successful financial training company (New Learning Developments) in New York City. Returning to London in 1999, he worked as a training consultant to financial services institutions, online brokerage houses, and the Ministry of Defense. He has published *Competing in Financial Markets* and several short stories. Currently, he is working on his first novel *Rape of the Aegean*.

Index

OTHER TITLES IN OUR FINANCE AND FINANCIAL MANAGEMENT COLLECTION

John A. Doukas, Old Dominion University, *Editor*

- *Numbers that Matter: Learning What to Measure to Achieve Financial Success in Your Business* by Evan Bulmer
- *Competing in Financial Markets: How to Play With the Best of Them* by Philip Cooper
- *Global Mergers and Acquisitions, Second Edition: Combining Companies Across Borders, Volume I* by Abdol S. Soofi and Yuqin Zhang
- *Global Mergers and Acquisitions, Second Edition: Combining Companies Across Borders, Volume II* by Abdol S. Soofi
- *Risk and Win!: A Simple Guide to Managing Risks in Small and Medium-Sized Organizations* by John Harvey Murray
- *Essentials of Financial Risk Management: Practical Concepts for the General Manager* by Rick Nason and Brendan Chard
- *Essentials of Enterprise Risk Management: Practical Concepts of ERM for General Managers* by Rick Nason and Leslie leming
- *Frontiers of Risk Management, Volume I: Key Issues and Solutions* by Dennis Cox
- *Frontiers of Risk Management, Volume II: Key Issues and Solutions* by Dennis Cox
- *The Art and Science of Financial Modeling* by Anurag Singal
- *Escape from the Central Bank Trap, Second Edition: How to Escape From the $20 Trillion Monetary Expansion Unharmed* by Daniel Lacalle

Announcing the Business Expert Press Digital Library

Concise e-books business students need for classroom and research

This book can also be purchased in an e-book collection by your library as

- a one-time purchase,
- that is owned forever,
- allows for simultaneous readers,
- has no restrictions on printing, and
- can be downloaded as PDFs from within the library community.

Our digital library collections are a great solution to beat the rising cost of textbooks. E-books can be loaded into their course management systems or onto students' e-book readers.
The **Business Expert Press** digital libraries are very affordable, with no obligation to buy in future years. For more information, please visit **www.businessexpertpress.com/librarians**. To set up a trial in the United States, please email **sales@businessexpertpress.com**.

CPSIA information can be obtained
at www.ICGtesting.com
Printed in the USA
FSHW011631091019
62788FS